STAINED GLASS SOULS

Stained Glass Souls

Vic

enjoy

your new friend

Don Queen

Donald Queen

Copyright © 2016 by Donald Queen.

Library of Congress Control Number: 2016910333
ISBN: Hardcover 978-1-5245-1202-6
       Softcover 978-1-5245-1201-9
       eBook 978-1-5245-1200-2

All rights reserved. No part of this book may be reproduced or transmitted in any form or by any means, electronic or mechanical, including photocopying, recording, or by any information storage and retrieval system, without permission in writing from the copyright owner.

Any people depicted in stock imagery provided by Thinkstock are models, and such images are being used for illustrative purposes only.
Certain stock imagery © Thinkstock.

Print information available on the last page.

Rev. date: 07/13/2016

To order additional copies of this book, contact:
Xlibris
1-888-795-4274
www.Xlibris.com
Orders@Xlibris.com

Contents

Honeysuckle 1
The Walk 2
Invisible Trees 9
The Edge of Wonder 10
I'm Paddling As Fast As I Can 11
The leap 13
Wings 15
Seasoned 16
The Drive To Taos 17
The Miracle Mile 19
Soft Organic Smudges 21
Thoughts Like Water 22
The Abbey, the Nebula and Songs of the Soul 24
The Greatest Show On Earth 29
Con-fused 30
Rotting Thread 31
Thoughts of Suicide 32
Victim 33
The Coffin 35
Dancing in the Dark 36
Pardon Me While I Die Here 38
Maximum Security 39
Hard Walled Valleys 41
Grasping at Shadows 42
Strands 44
Stained Glass Souls 45
Wake-up 46
My Woods 49
Hot Wax 50
Keystone Block 51
Bloody Thoughts and Clay 52
Lies 54
Summer Rain 55

Lust for Life	56
Watching the Road	58
US Highways 60 and 63	59
Fluorescent Kisses	61
Sweet Woman and Shore Lines	63
Dream Dancers	64
Diamonds, Silvers Of Glass And Other Shiny Things	65
Relief Somewhere in the Seventies	69
A Korean War Casualty	74
Bottomless Boxes	75
Deep Freeze	76
Sitting on a Cabin Porch at the Foot of an Old Mountain	77
Delicate Threads	78
The Diner	79
Causeways	81
Blame It On the Hot Coffee	83
Pale Dreams	84
The Flower	86
Habits	88
EBB and Flow	89
The Lie	93
Peeking Thomas	94
Dripping to the Flow	95
God in a Box	97
The Angel's Prize	99
I Am	100
A Spiritual Experience	101
Expectations and New Awakenings	103
ReCreation	106
The Calling	107
And So Are We	109
A Just Right Spring Day	110
A Soul in Disguise	111

    These stories and poems have entertained and befuddled me at times, but often these scribbles have saved my sanity, if not my life. These meanderings both fun, painful and freeing will be in five categories, though some could almost fit anywhere. A mix of my humor and anguish that I often had to force out and at other times couldn't stop the process. This collection of words ranges from fear to love, from the creative process to nature and Spirituality. These choices come from about a thirty-five year span. From the point of setting down the alcohol and drugs and trudging through years of anxiety and depression.

    Watch out for the second chapter. <u>Mud, Molasses and Stained Glass Souls.</u> This chapter shows my struggles to get past my self-centered fears. Don't linger in that mire, I almost didn't make it through the illusions. I just want to show that sometimes insanity and stupidity are on the same side of the path. If that crazy chapter is too dark just run to the next one. I don't need to live in it any more, though I don't want to forget were I've come from. I just hope someone can find something in here to embrace or let go of.

With love
Don Queen

    I want to thank my wife Bobbie Jo for being with me these sixteen plus years. I want to acknowledge my sister Paula and stepsister Janelle for being in my life. And all those friends that have continued to be friends even after they came to know me. And thanks to the twelve step programs and all the people in them. May we continue to be there for each other. I want to thank my new yoga family for helping me relax and stand strong as I can in each challenge. Each breath is a miracle. And to all my children, whether you are biological, stepchildren or foster girls, wow, you taught me more than you could know

    And a special thanks to Stephanie Pifer-Stone and her husband Rick, my Light Sabers.

Love you all
Don Queen

HONEYSUCKLE

My nose suckled the honeysuckle
My toes tapped the hardened trail
My woes somehow lost their muscle
I'm on down the road wagging my tail ...

The Walk

I'm going for a walk today
Out past concrete and blacktop
Down through the woods
Between the preened pastures of the links
And trash at the landfill
Between carded scores and discarded unwanted's
Stepping carefully on loose stones and fallen limbs
Around downed trees
Bare brush and bared thorns
Through the rich smell of dirt and decaying leaves
Past fast rabbits
And nutty squirrels

As I go lower
The earth opens sections of a solid rock hillside
To show meaning
Exposing a harder existence
With car and truck sized chunks
That have pulled away over many ages
Hardly grains of sand in my life
One of these separating gashes allows a gradual path
Through the dormant vegetation
On down to a guarding shield
Of twisted gnarled branches and undergrowth
One last slap on my open face
And I break through to the tracks
To the almost level ground
Of manmade canyons and filled gullies
Where big boxes blow by on clanking wheels

I walk past this open road
East deeper into the valley

Stained Glass Souls

Just above the creek
Several deer stand looking at me-
I enter the long clearing-
White tails flag as the herd vanishes into the woods
When I move on a handful of robins
Hop from bushes
They check the cool ground for life
Pecking past the surface
Seeing me they shy back with a flutter
I walk on by with a smile
On above the water
Until an easy slope gives me access

Erosion must have toppled the tree
Roots and limbs on either end
The smooth bone white of this sycamore
Has darkened with death
Thirty feet of front row seat
A backless pew before the altar
I carefully cross the stream on rocky stones
Water gurgles past my feet
I sit with pencil and paper

The stream narrows and widens as the bed changes
Sometimes speaking
Sometimes quiet in those deceptive pools
That pulls me to my soul
To connect with my surroundings
An elemental direction of Law
If it's dammed beware!
Power good or bad can take us out of here
Or make us more aware
The earth in its spinning shows the sun higher
The fire in me raises desire
I scribble notes of gratitude

The sun and wind on this second day of January
A beautiful reprieve that helps me relieve
The pull of hibernation
The invigorating cold water warms my thoughts
The dead tree holds me above the damp ground

Donald Queen

The wind carries a fresh sweetness
As it continues to caress my face and
Tenderly arouse the slowed life around me-
I breath in each moment-
I watch two leaves converge on a narrow rivulet
Speeding and spinning onto a deeper body
Now they move gently with a hidden current

I am!
I am a child of God
I am a brother
A friend
A husband
A father
A lover
I AM ALIVE!

A woodpecker hammers past the surface
Echoing in my mind
I fold up my notebook
Put away the pencil
To carefully walk flat rocks across the stream
Then I backtrack up the slope
Up the long clearing
Past the robins
Over the iron rails
I follow another path now
A deer trail
Up a different hillside
Through the drowsy trees and brush
Past a few busy squirrels
Over and around the glass and tin and paper and aluminum and plastic
I pull my way up one last steep grade
To a gravel road that I take to the top of the hill

I look out over my meditation
Limestone outcropping look like scabbed over sores
The large sycamores like bare bones
The rails and ties show a stitched scar through the middle of Eden
If I hadn't just come from there

Stained Glass Souls

I wouldn't be able to make out the traces of the stream

The cloudless blue winter sky brightens
The crowded families of trees raise their limbs to freedom
Several vees of geese honk over the valley
What does all this mean to me?

A bell rings from the tower
Counting down the hours
I walk back to where I started
Lighter in my head
Warmer in my heart
I turn the key
I'm on my way home!

SOFT ORGANIC SMUDGES

INVISIBLE TREES

I'm sitting here waiting for words to grow
Special words picked out of the air
I write knowing they're going to show
Here on the paper if I'm aware
I reach up and pluck fresh, ripe choices
That hang on stout invisible trees
It's nice finding fruit with voices
That help us laugh, cry, and to be free
Once digested seeds drop to the ground
The same chance as acorns to germinate
The roots take and limbs are heaven bound
Again, I pick food for my paper plates.

THE EDGE OF WONDER

I'm sitting on the edge of wonder
Like a little boy swinging his feet off the end of a dock
Watching turtle heads go under as he skips another rock

Is that noise a distant thunder
Or just my heart beating like that little boy's?
A mirror to the lonely stalking hunter
The allusive prey so dear

Ain't easy to satisfy this hunger
But I'll be keeping pockets of rocks for each day
As I sit on the edge of wonder
Like a little boy at play

I'm Paddling As Fast As I Can

If I could make a picture with words
I would memorize moments
I'd file organized letters
To call them up at need
And as the miseries sneak up
Like they sometimes do
I could pull out a new morning
Or sunset
As I please

And when I'm a tear dropping fool
Like I sometimes am
I could call on a desert
To soak up the flood
To keep me from drowning
On my knees

And when I become the king again
As I surely will
I could pull out a peaceful blue-green pond
Surrounded by the smell of fresh-cut lawn
Shaded by oaks and willows
And spiny honey locust trees
Decorated by heart-shaped leave of several red buds
A few young spruces
With bottle brush needles
And pinecone seeds

I could call on little ducklings
To follow mama
And she could parade the cute fuzzy balls
Away from me

And as they float quietly out of my realm
I would know regardless of appearance
Their tiny webbed feet
Are paddling like hell
And even with such strong imprints
Most likely
Not all these darling little birds
Will continue to be able to flee

And when I can't make sense
of a situation
With words
I could pour down a crystal clear spring
To run over my doubts and frustrations
The stones and boulders of my mind
And as the water swirls and bubbles
I could see through
The fresh cool relief
Or watch a fallen leaf
Twist and dive
Through the pools and rapids
The channels of my life

On down the rivers
On down to the seas

And when the waters vaporize
Raise up to become clouds
To float in the heavens
With worded moments memorized
I can call them back to me
As I please

The Leap

Sometimes when the poets gone
And I'm wandering through the mush
I think I've done something wrong
Then try to push way too much

Rhyming words is not enough
I need the heart to come along
Yea, to learn the artist touch
I must loose the inner song

If I let the throbbing brain
Relax and trust the poet's voice
I know I can stop the game
Acknowledging I have a choice

So, quiet now, stop the noise
Learn to know the gnawing pains
I let myself feel the joys
See the truth behind the chains

I shine my light on my friends
Nurture the love we have sown
Much too soon our flicker ends-
Some sins are way too overblown

I paint pictures on the winds
And place words like cobblestones
I take the clay in my hands
And feel the poet in my bones

A leap is more than just the words
The sun ain't the center of my life

DONALD QUEEN

I like the light and energy
But darkness holds an inner key
Balance is eternity
My fulcrum will be the death of me
Or my life!

WINGS

The eyes of the hawk
Sharp as his talons
Eagerly searches the ground
As he floats on high

Wobbling as they walk
Short wings for balance
Penguins easily soar unbound
Using water for their sky

I continue to stalk
Sharpen my talents
As creative streams are found
I need no wings to fly

Seasoned

In this morning sky of gray and blue
With leaves the color of blood and death
Where life is put on hold
Or left to go to other things
I sometimes wonder why I hope
Or just want to go to sleep
I sometimes struggle in these smells of rotting life
That falls and settles year upon year upon year

The cold and snow will blow
To numb my trust
Will push me to the inner chamber
Where smoke and fire will make me taste
Each memory bit by bit
Make me savor each loving touch
Or spit hate and anger back into the flames
To pop and crackle till it billows up in the breeze
Or mixes with the ashes
To be shoveled out to free me to hear
The angelic songs that flutter in my soul

To rake my mind and pile changed thoughts
So I can run and jump to my hearts desire
In the cold and snow and fallen dreams
Oh, to roll and play
Till the coming greens begin another season …

The Drive To Taos

Remember our drive to Taos?
I didn't expect that much traffic coming out of Sante Fe.
And after cresting the mountain pass we could see
The lights spread across the valley.
It seemed so magical.
But when we descended through the little towns
All we could see were fast food joints,
Bars and filling stations.
As we continued north, I was glad to elevate again.
We twisted through the passes and hugged close
To the carved mountains.
Remember stopping to see and hear the river
Of melted snow that ran heartily down
And stopping to see and feel how close the stars are there?
I held you tight knowing how special these moments are.
Remember how we hurried through Taos
Deciding to look for a ski resort?
We stalked our way twisting higher
Our headlights showing more and more snow covering
The dark ground and trees.
We expected something around every curve.
Occasionally we passed a lone house or failed business.
Finally, we could see lights on the side of the peaks.
There were homes anchored to the cold rocks
Far beyond any dream I could afford.
As we drove into a snow packed parking lot
I wondered how people could survive such folly.
Remember how we took a cold stroll up to some shops
On the shoveled sidewalk?
All that was still open was the tavern.
We glanced in the window at the happy, red or
Black eyes of the occupants.

As we huddled close we could hear the laughter,
The boasts and whispers coming from the bar.
As we shivered back to the car,
I felt some sense of accomplishment,
Even though we only stood and looked
At the snow-covered playground.
And as we eased back toward town I thought
About returning with a deep plastic card
And a wad of cash.
When we finally made it back to Taos
It was about midnight.
We parked just off the main road to look in the
Dimly lit windows of the art galleries.
My inspiration was even greater
Than living in some chateau on a mountain
Sliding around with skis hooked to my feet.
I then longed to live on and ride the slopes of creativity.
I longed to drive the slick roads of wonder.
And God, I remember
No dream or scheme could touch what I saw
In that little town's windows.
Clay, stone, metal, wood and paint.
Works truly Divinely Inspired.
The art filled me with Awe.
I ache as I doubt my abilities to weave such works.
I push back the tears of my want-to-be's.
The desire to become all that I can
Only serves to torture me
When I live in the fear of not letting myself try.

THE MIRACLE MILE

I got caught in one of those movies-again last night!
The good guy and the bad dilemma
You know, where he follows his heart
Where life comes down to a competition or a test
Down to the wire or on the ropes
Where everything depends on your faith-your hope
You know those choices where you don't give up
Even if there seems to be no way in hell
You can accomplish that desire
No way to become more than you are
Because, so many dreams have come and gone
And you either turned your back in fear
Or maybe you did stick to the end
All the way to disaster
This movie had me balling like a baby
For the realities faced and the dream that still shined
In the eyes of the beholder
We know in these movies there is a chance
Down to the tick of the last second on the clock!
You know, when they hang in there till the miracle happens!
If you're like me your laughing and crying at the same time
Pumping your fist in the air or
Clapping like this is some kind of reality
So glad for their success at following that dream
Where we feel that glow in our whole put-together
We feel that deep seated joy
Even though we've walked too many green miles
Where the good guys are fried
And the only remains are buried or
Blown away in the wind
So now I come back to that feeling in my heart
That want for hope

Even though I can see, and taste, and feel
There is no way in hell
I can get beyond the past failures and run-a-way's
But you also know how, despite our fear
We can wake the next morning
Climb from bed
Pray to God
And walk right on out the door
Ready for the day
And for some reason there's smiles on our faces…

Soft Organic Smudges

I've sketched the shadows line-by-line
Crosshatched to infinity
I've filled the night with broad side strokes
Smudged white to gray and gray to midnight
I've teetered on the edge of the page-
Or was it the universe?
Only to have the moon and stars meld
To glow over my shoulder
To guide the charcoal in my hand
Let the cool ember burn into the paper
Leaving my ego in the dust ...

Thoughts Like Water

Thoughts like water
Flowing
Rippling around and through my emotions
Running in my heart and mind
I dip my hands in the wet waves of pictures
That splash on my palms
Through my fingers
Images run in rivulets like tears
Pain-laughter-gratitude
Pooling and sinking into the earth
Looking like the remnants of a spring shower
Stones glisten with whispers of doubt and hope
I grab at the gooey jewels
I pick at the sinking thoughts
But all I have is muddied fingers
Looking like ink stained hands
I stand numbed
As the thoughts soak into the thirsty ground
Almost quiet now the
Scattered pictures whimper into obscurity
To be walked on
Like the left overs of a morning dew
Too soon to disappear
As a mirage
As a forgotten negative in the
Bottom of a old worn out shoe box
But as the day lightens I think I can see
Little morsels of condensation
Raise up as clouds to sprinkle
Or thoughts spring back through the earth's crust
To bring fractured pictures
To the four corners

Stained Glass Souls

In a universal language of thought
Filtered pictures rejoin to flow
Around our little spin in the universe
To rush down mountain streams
Or wash in on waves
Glistening on the beaches
Shimmering
Bubbling
Reviving our bodies
Our heart
Flowing like water through our thoughts

The Abbey, the Nebula and Songs of the Soul

There is a crack, just above the cross, that hangs on the new green paint
A bulge in the plaster adds an appropriate flaw on this old abbey's wall
I expected sleep to come easy
But sometimes anticipation thrills my thoughts
Steals my heart
I've come for newness in a brotherhood of strength
I've come for jewels from a Father-Good-of Love
I want to be all that I am
Ready for the next miracle
Sometimes I want to stay awake forever
So not to miss the twinkles in the night

A splash of Holy in a tranquil colored wine
A slice of sustenance taken in on the tip of the soul
Eyebrows arched with deep furrowed lines
As singing praises flow

The charted sky might divulge my next lodestone or pyrite glitter
As our sun burns someone's back on the other side of the world
I watch other stars-
Are they still alive
Or just fading visions from the last light beams of dead bodies?
They hiss across the universe
Across the void that gives depth to eternity
Are these embers giving a last breath of warmth
To the dark spaces between fire, rock and ice?
Billows of clouded dust and gases
Star nurseries
Nebula colored like an aurora's shimmering lights
More immense than structure rainbows

Stained Glass Souls

More intense than a wavering oasis that isn't there
Just hot air

I choose this night as my universal song
With lyrics of relativity
Words of Honor and Awe
Laughter and heartache
Oh, to share my song with angels
To release born again shame
Moments of crystalline words dancing off my cords
Streaming past my flapping tongue and sputtering lips
Like wind on clover
Or gales on the jagged cliffs and cottonwoods
Music to guide the brave
Or sooth the petrified weak
Music to tap a toe or throb your temple
Till the blood spews through your heart like a red spring of courage
Music to plant dreams by
To sink your teeth into
Oh to here my soul on the willow's thin reeds of wisdom
Or on aspen leaves twisting
Waving good-by to the evening
Living in the motion of genetic memory

I've known songs with the deep tones of black holes
I know the pull of darkness
I see it manipulate its surroundings
I can smell and taste the elements of raw energy and dead matter
I feel the hot and cold press together
I hear the hum of ancient atoms rubbing against themselves
Pushing-pulling vibrating to a drone
I'm drawn deep into the collection
Deep to a frantic sleep
Caged in a dimple in time and space
If my number isn't up I may leak out
Maybe to a realm of angelic domain
I may wiggle and crawl through a worm hole
Back to where I started
Or forward to where I ain't
I could grab a string and the whole image would come unraveled
To spread me light years across the cosmos

To the clear ethereal music of glittering emeralds and diamonds

The night sky can be seen in layers
Poked and probed for answers
Past the fear and frustration of self-pity
I peel away the skins of my thoughts
To the skins of my perceptions
To give clarity to reality and parity to this existence

Chosen as a new beginning this day comes as usual
With a myriad of faces and confusing schemes
I learn with life hitting me with hail stones
Or a gentle rain on my weeded garden
Oh, to hear the songs of my heart
On the altar of a quiet mind
Give release to friends and family
To be open to miracles for me to find

Spit on those hands
Swing that hammer
Sing that song
Let your Soul spin out as New Born Light!

MUD MOLASSES AND STAINED GLASS SOULS

THE GREATEST SHOW ON EARTH

He cried about the bumps
The bruises
The terrible pains
Waved them in my face
Like some kind of trophy
Bubbling with pride inside
A three ring circus
Feelings and thoughts
Walk the high wire
Tame the lion
Mostly run around like a clown
Try to put the fire out
With a bucket full of confetti

Con-fused

I don't know when the wick became a fuse
When the glowing flame of passion became a sickening hiss
A low sizzling, sparkle heading for an eruption
When did this mutable wax body
Build up all this drama from miss used power?

When did it go from that gentle flicker
To that serpent sound of warning?
That forked tongue of fear

Can I pinch that fuse?
Change my fate?
And still maintain a fire
To push me back from the edge of the dark canyon of doubt
To show my flame to the wounded and dying
To show that shame is just another distraction

Shame, like guilt is just a warning sign
Not something to wrap my life in
Only to smother any chance I have
To walk hand in hand with my family and friends

How do I change back from this stick of dynamite
To that mutable, lovable haloed fire?
How do I defuse this ire
Bent on destruction?

Rotting Thread

Dangling like daggers on rotting thread
Tied and forgotten till all my dread
Has vanished from my memory
Like my birth

From my memory of my worth
In this tangled existence of gain
And suffering
Of chains and buffering pain with lies
Ignoring the rusted blades
That were tied with hate
Sated with resentment and revenge
Each knot soaked
In the blood of generations
Of regenerated payments
Dangling in the dark closet

The walls of the house
Painted so nicely
Decorated so wisely
With beautiful abstracts
And impressionistic intent
A compressionist relentless bent
To look good in the front rooms
And front yard
Trying hard to forget what's hanging
Over old coats and collected reminders
Collected binders to the past
Sidewinders to the last remains of decency
The last strains of dependency
On old worn out ways

Thoughts of Suicide

In thoughts of suicide
I think of others
Of sisters and brothers
Of ammunition passed down
From moms and dads

I think of sadness
I think of madness
Of misread instructions
Mislead inductions
Into halls of fame
Or walls of shame
I think of habits
Concealed in rights
Revealed in wrongs
Passed on as
Our only choices

What with the way
Of our world and all
Who can blame us?
Who can name us?
As one of the chosen
Or one of the frozen
Sliding across the day
Unable to thaw out the disasters
That are our Divine Rights
Or our Sublime Wrongs.

VICTIM

He floated on the ocean waves
Far too often going under
Ages and ages, day after day
Splashing in his lonesome wander

One morning he crested high
Saw the green hills of land
He was determined he would try
To stand on something solid again

As he neared he saw the rocks
It was much too late to get away
He braced for the on coming shocks
And searched a deeper way to pray

When crashing to the jagged shore
Wave after wave, hit again and again
From nothing to a constant roar
He thought the assault would never end

On the backside of a slippery crag
Pondering why life did him wrong
As the undertow would push and drag
He often cried a sad lonely song

Gradually the water pulled back
Giving him time to rest his hold
Searching relief from the next attack
Shivering from the soggy cold

He crouched behind a stony wall
Braced for the oncoming tide

Donald Queen

And as the waves began to fall
He knew he'd found a place to hide

Each day between the ebb and flow
He peeked from behind his curse
Afraid that if tried to go
He'd venture into something worse

He braced for every onslaught
And slept when the waves were clear
Convinced that he'd been taught
He had to live his time in fear

When down the beach on either side
The rocks had crumbled into sand
As he sat there trying to hide
He could be walking on green land

THE COFFIN

The dawn has come
And it's too late to make a difference
The whispers have grown to screams
And I sit here like a thief
Will I burn today
Or will a wooden stake anchor me to the coffin?

Last night I splashed through the blackness
Seeking another climax
Fondling dreams and reality
Sticking my fangs in strange places
Innocence came
Looked me in the eyes
I forced here down
Caressing the soft cheeks
I searched the supple neck for the juiciest place
Piercing flesh
I sucked out the salty life

Pulling my cloak around me
I left the victim to whimper
Alone in the dark

Now the dawn has come
I sit here like a monster
But I'm only human
And somehow I think that's worse

Dancing in the Dark

The door was locked
Shades and curtains held back the sun
Three lit candles
Burned in different corners
I sat in the dark in the remaining one.
Spacey music drifted through my head
I can't take a chance-
A sad hostage of shadows from the dead.
A dim light struggles through the smoke
Side to side, flickers tease for attention
Apparitions begin a sickly dance.
Pleas echo in my mind

My voice crumbles to the floor.
Fear sinks deeper in this great expanse.
My chest bangs harder
I think to rush the door,
But I'm curious about these grim reminders.
A chill intensifies my sweaty pores.
The voices of strange friends and familiar strangers
Twist my senses and thoughts
I'm panicked into schemes.
I flirt with my ancient master-
it forces me to dance.
Sickening spins and leaps
Pressed close to my long, dead dreams
And the skeletal knocking of my stupidity.
The music bleeds from the walls
To run out beneath my feet
Causing my moves to be as a puppet's.
The candles burn to nothing
Darkness closes in like a black fog

Stained Glass Souls

My blood dance continues
Till I fall exhausted to the ground.
I am forced to wallow in the thick, morbid songs
Until all my expectations die
And my heart is the only sound.

Pardon Me While I Die Here

Here's that muddled puddle of molasses again
Oh what a sin
Stuck in this pool
A fool to nature
Slowed to a raw numbness
Trying to call out
But forgetting the names

And the dark goo has my lips glued
Mumbling something about fear
With meaningless prattle
Oh what a battle
What a dark life we war
When we are unsure of ourselves
And God and the Law of the land

Please give me a hand
And I'll stand on the edge
And cleanse my heart and mind
Of the destructions we wrest
From the suicidal attempts at salvation
In this meaningless self-assembled damnation
Of you and me and galaxies

Maximum Security

The window hangs on the transparent wall
Clouded light shines through to fall
On the floor to show the shadow of bars

A reminder of a new morning in the cell
The bed post notched, another day, oh well
Do only I see the shackles that mortify?

The invisible tether rubs thin skin raw
Imaginary rats and roaches hungrily gnaw
At thoughts on the shelves in open jars

Paranoia on the prowl with teeth of fear
A reflecting window in each fat tear
Falling from eyes beginning to calcify

I stumble on feet that feel like lead
Back to the morbid comfort of my bed
To dream of the loneliness of the stars

The astral lights come near to show
They are only tunnels letting out a glow
Not some cold distant termini

I put in a finger to plug a hole
Wondering if on the other side they know
There is energy leaking from their scars

Trying to pull myself from this dream
I am stuck, being sucked into the beam
Surely, I'm finally, going to die

Donald Queen

No longer night, just a trace of day
Hide and seek is the game to play
We run for cover but, not too far

A boy in a bush, a girl behind a tree
One kid was camouflaged, very hard to see
And I am crouched behind a lie

The counting stops, the search is on
Though all the players had gone
Gone on to be the people they are

As the shadows melt into the dark
I strike stones for one last spark
Searching for another alibi

I wake from hell, jump from my bed
I see there's nothing else to be said

Hard Walled Valleys

I've stood in the dark
Just around the corner
Too near the dead end streets
And people on knees
In shadowy alleys

Craving another spark
Playing a foreigner
I hear the dreaded beat
Of echoes in these
Hard walled valleys

Bedding with a mark
Slinking past the warner's
Fears, knowing they'll cheat
Doing what they please
Faking ecstasy

I've looked in the stark
Eyes of the mourner's
Tears, betting they'll repeat
The same old sleaze
And blame their families

Life can be a lark
I pray past the scorners
So dear and so sweet
It ain't easy to believe
My problem is me!

Grasping at Shadows

As I struggled for a reason
Grasping at shadowy images
I clawed through the dark forms
They were senseless
It was like they needed me to give meaning
Fingers through water or sand
With no texture, no weight
Just shadows of fears
Old battles thru years of drama
Dragged along with me
Because I didn't know better
Well maybe I knew
I just couldn't get past myself
I couldn't trust that Spirit
Had better plans than me running around
Looking for more reasons
To be the center of my little universe
A tight ball of spinning nothing
Shadows of ignorance
Not trusting, afraid to care
Lost in humanities battle with itself
So many candles and night lights
Individual light sources
Casting figures from their thoughts
Dancing off the walls and ceilings
Scary wanderings bouncing off my imagination
Childish memories of something under the bed
Or peeking from the closet
Headlights flash across the room
A raccoon or stray dog in the yard
Clanking cans or rustling trash bags
The settling of the old house popping and moaning

Stained Glass Souls

A mouse gnawing
These shadows that run round my head
Screaming without any real sound
It's like dreaming
Only the moment seems so awake and real

Now I settle back in my faith
Ignoring the commotion
No substance here
Just thoughts on the edge of insanity

STRANDS

Doubt whistled easily through me
Like wind on a screen door
But, faiths tightly woven strands
Held back creatures of the night

The door rattled and a weak shadow
Snuck over the floor
Something dark in its hands
Hidden from the moons dull light

My mind fluttered in the breeze
As darkness moved slowly in
Looking like some slimy leach
Crawling after my soul

Fear quickly moved in
Like it's shadowy kin
But just couldn't reach in
Onto it's needed goal

And still the screen door rattled
And the shadow filled the frame
So I dodged the clammy touch
Not sure what the dark might do

Yes, my human mind battled
But faith doesn't play games
And shadows can't eat much--
The creature couldn't get through!

Stained Glass Souls

Fired into glass

Transformed from
A coarse, shifting beginning
Colored or crystalline

Cut and held into place
By heavy, flexible lead

Patterns of life and character
Designs of our souls

Some panes are brittle
Easily broken
Some fade or bleed

Glass and lead of the earth

Pieced together

Ready for the light

WAKE-UP

It is like I'm searching for that explosion of light
That sudden awakening
That knowing
Trying to have what Bill W. had
And all I can do is continue to chop the wood
And carry the water
All I can do is be the best me I can be
I've had my visions and dreams
Moments of clarity
And the feelings and knowing's
That I'm on the right path
I can search for the truths in my life
And wonder at the wonders in this existence
Do I kick against the pricks
Or cease fighting anything or anybody?
Do I look for that One Path
Or do I search for the best me I can be?
Do I come to that place of acceptance
And pulsate my love to everything good and bad?
Can I stand in awe at the wonders
And know that either there is a God or there isn't?
What is my choice to be?
Do I trust in Love or do I fight at the angry illusions
Of resentment and self pity?
What is this bubble around me that distorts my vision
That makes me think I have to be more than I am?
What are these insane thoughts that have me crying in my sleep?

Wake-up!

THE FOURTH TIME IS A CHARM

My Woods

Eager eyes
Easy smile

I watch deep from my woods
My forest of darkness
Oh please wander from the path
Stand tangled in the underbrush

Look at the way her tongue moved
Is she making a statement
Or dampening dry lips?

Wild creatures of habit
Beast or human, creepy crawlies
Fast little snakes and lizards

Such a gentle touch
Just a brush against the arm
Ah, it tingled to my marrow

Be careful in the berry patch
Take it slow
The thorns can rip and tear

Hot Wax

In the cover
Of a dark moon
Time slowed
To the moment
Sounds of the night
On this summer swoon
Keep kisses of passion
Muffled
Till too late
To stop the rush
Of the tender embrace
That grew to the grind
Of joined souls
Fate or folly
Will rise with the sun
Too late to shed goals
Of unintentional Eternity
Too late
To shut our eyes
Or extinguish the flame
That shortened the candle
That drips hot wax
As the jumping fire
Creates funny shadows
On the shuttered room

Keystone Block

Sitting on that keystone block
Bolstered with sandbag dreams
The place you call your home
With parachute walls held up
By erratic beams

Down to the end of your rope
Coiled like a serpent round your feet
Thought you'd make it on your own
That a hint of pink would make it easy

Now you hide under your cowl
And those loose fitting cloths
You're able to hear the whispers—
Unable to muffle the screams

Meanwhile on the other side
You're tied to yourself
With unraveling lines
That virginal stare keeps you busy

While your soul patiently waits—
For the release

Bloody Thoughts and Clay

Axle grease is used again
Smeared on the canvas
To swirl and blend
With bloody thoughts
And yellow clay
What's being shown
On this smeared display?

She stands there exposed
But I can't get past
The emotional pain
Naked to the heart
But my blind mind sees
Only lines of suspicion
And carnal greed

She warms her hands
On that fleshy fire
Pulls it in to lift desire
Splits the mask of
Good and evil
And spills out her soul
To ease that pain

Angels and demons
In this mortal dance
Pushing and pulling
To win her name
So she scoops the clay
In those bloody hands
Taking one more chance

Stained Glass Souls

And will wake
Before morning
To slip away ...

LIES

I stroked her tired head
She slowly went to sleep
A lullaby came to mind
I closed red eyes instead
Thinking hope not often kind

We dreamed the pain be gone
With the rising of the day
Pulling warm covers near
We thought change would come
That our love was too dear

She saw me try to stop it
Make her think I was
Rubbing sleep from my eyes
But it ran on down to my lips
Like all my other lies

Summer Rain

Magical drops of summer rain
Glittering sequins in the night
Gradually wash away the pain
Easing the anger from our fight

The down pour mingles with my own
I wonder if I should walk away—
Or hold misery etched in stone
How many more acts in this play?

A dim light flickers through the blinds
I was afraid to venture in
Oh, the things we hope not to find
Why do we fight when no one wins?

Now I wander through empty rooms
As blunders rumble through me
Each step darkens a lonely gloom
I look but I don't want to see

Remnants of a worn, hidden past
With faded pictures and lost dreams
We thought things made our love last
And was something for bargaining

A candle by the empty bed
Burning with a waxy odor
Awakens shadows in my head
Damn, I wish my heart was colder!

LUST FOR LIFE

No foliage to stop me, I see the underside
The quiet slumber. It's almost embarrassing
To look at the naked elder—the twisted limbs
And gnarly knobs of that Noble Oak

Worn wooden slates, fragile rungs to nowhere
A few two-by's dangle, remnants of a house
Traces of nests of birds and humans
They migrate in their own seasons

A vine hangs twisted like a frozen snake
Coiled in the limbs of a young oak
As a child I would cut that living rope
To swing out over the world ...

Now, I sit, watch stringy shredded bark
Separate and bend and turn away
From the reddish-brown meandering vine that's
Pulling, crushing, sucking life-for life

Some miles east of here, near the Missouri
Yards and yards of circled, coiled vines
Are piled in a heap around a sycamore
The tree thin and tall, straight as an arrow

The vine had grown-wrapped-twisted
Wound round the slick bark tree
Too much snow and growth, the vine
Crumpled, shearing the week lower branches

Looking like a dropped skirt around ankles
Showing creamy smooth skin to the sun

The remaining top limbs spread as in surprise
The sycamore was released of its serpent

The vine was pulled down by its own weight
Pulled down, because of its lust for life

I watch from a wood chipped path, knowing
Given a chance, this stand could be a forest!

Watching the Road

We were driving through strange territory
She sat talking to the car window
Did she need the company of her reflection
Or the strength of her echo off the glass?

She whispered shy words
To her side of the world
Leaving me to watch the road
And wonder what she was mumbling about

So I thought about this new chance
How we needed more than change
Melting down the phones with passion
Listening to Melissa and the Eagles

Walking the trail between
The palisades and the muddy river
Ripping ourselves from the past
Looking through stained glass and steamy mirrors

US Highways 60 and 63

We had changed seats at the crossing
The top was open
The seat was tilted back
I was in the middle world
Between sleep and where are we
My eyes would open to blue and fluffy
And I'd float back off again
A screech, like the magnified sound of
A fingernail on a chalk board
Followed by a deep churning rumble
Irritated me awake
We were riding beside a freight train
Parallel roads to different worlds
We gradually inched past the noise
I mellowed and laid may head back
To float off again

But I found myself searching
The sky for dreams instead
In the evening blue
The waxing moon faced east
Toward two coarse looking clouds-
I thought of soft sandpaper-
A little wisp of condensation

Hung between the two rough puffs
It looked like a clamp
Maybe a bobby pin
Ready to hold hair out of our eyes
I glanced at the road
Looked past the pair of dice
Hanging from the rearview mirror

Donald Queen

The wisp had changed to an angel
Long robbed
Magnificent, muscular towering wings
Guarding the space between the larger clouds
Its hands were spread
Offering safe passage
I looked back to the earth
A grassy pasture lined with cedars and oaks
Protected four horses
I followed layers of hills to the horizon
Blue and silver rested atop green and gold
My eyes found a calm, shaded lake
And added water of their own

We passed a stand of pines
Dark pushed away the day
I looked beyond the rearview mirror
And we rode on into paradise . . .

Fluorescent Kisses

A midnight ride takes us to a shelter house
In a deserted park
The gravel crunches till we come to a stop
We step into the night
A heavy breeze rustles through the tall grass and the trees

We search the stars for direction
A small river flows nearby
Picnic tables become a covered grandstand
To watch the show
The fireflies outnumber the stars
The speckled sky is no match
For the greenish-yellow bursts

The day had been hot, normal for July
The steady wind that tosses her hair
Blows away the mosquitoes and the troubles of the day

A sliver of moon hides just beyond the horizon
Giving more room for the stars
Letting the fireflies control the night
Our eyes adjust
We begin to see the spectacle

Beyond the river is tall grass
With a backdrop of willows and cottonwoods
Mesmerized by the noiseless, mellow explosions
I find, again
There is often more to something
That first meets the eye

The area is full of little neon strobes

Donald Queen

Taking my attention to a different level
With a whisper of a kiss and a gentle caress
I think we are glowing
The fireflies wink their understanding
The soundless mating calls fill the air
Our grandstand becomes a stage

Continuous flashes like miniature cameras
Record our moves as we spark in the night

Sweet Woman and Shore Lines

Please don't pinch me I'm not dreaming!
White caps on waves, water streaming
So many gulls feeding comically rude
Pelicans soaring surprisingly good
We sun and splash for natures powers
Spend hours stopping to smell the flowers
Steaming of glass from humidity at noon
Then a cool breeze on a midnight dune
That shoos away troubles for a night of bliss
Osprey that dive beneath the surface for fish
Bursting back out with a watery sheen
Impassioned beauty of a fisherman's dream
The blessing of trying to play too much
The good I get from her gentle touch
The comforting smell of her that lingers
Jelly fish floating watch out for stingers
Sweet woman's laugh from a playground swing
The woman helps me feel like a king
Glass-bottom boat, a sprinkle of rain
And a dolphin's dance on a watery plain
Spanish-moss drooping that live oaks hold
The sound of waves that perpetually fold
Sun sparkled gold ripples on the blue
A coast line drive when the day is through
Anchored sail boats with gently swaying masts
The gorgeous sunsets that too quickly pass

DREAM DANCERS

I won't forget the moonlight
How it softly lights your face
Like whispers from the sunshine
Just a few more hours away

The slow metallic rhythm
Of the old wound-up clock
Keeps us in this special moment
Where worry has to stop

You feel me watch you now
You dream a late night dance
Face to face, glide step for step
So graceful hand in hand

Tick, tick, tick--an easy beat
I hold you close, though loosely
We step and turn and shuffle
Then swirl apart like music

Notes afloat as cloud puffs
We flutter on like laughter
Moment by hour by moment
To return as bee to nectar

Our souls spin the passion dance
Love still grows in our soaring
We flow as one in your dream-
Till bird songs bring the morning

DIAMONDS, SILVERS OF GLASS AND OTHER SHINY THINGS

We spent the night splashing in moonlight

As it shimmered in on the sea

Like slivers of glass scattered in the past

Cut into my memory

The silver- white dancing little sprites

Had intended to be set free

But just couldn't pass from waters so vast

So they sparkle for eternity

Like stars in flight flicker dull and bright

A constant glow of hope for me

They're diamonds cast in the varied paths

Pressed by my memory

MISCELLANEOUS

MEANDERINGS

Relief
Somewhere in the Seventies

They told me I knocked like a cop
I didn't know whether to smile or apologize
Allie told them I was Mr. Natural
Looking through the window pane
This was to explain why I was staring
Out of two black holes in the center of my eyes
I don't know where I met Allie
She had convinced me I needed to meet some friends of hers
Tru and his wife Patsy
They lived in a big house just east of Westport
It's about a block over from Berdella's vacant lot
I sat on their scratchy sofa
It was either a dirty green
Or a brown that was moldy
The mirror over the mantel reflected
More than the contents of the house
And I had to pee

Squeezing my bladder
I tried to act like everything was fine
Tonight I drank beer to settle my stomach
And to give me something familiar to hold onto
I couldn't get back out of the sofa
If I hadn't seen all the flaws
I might have been able to crawl
Up the steps without direction
Tru was a judge's son
But the weeds got too high
So he sat at the table picking out seeds
Picking up crumbs
The scales were heavy either way

Mainly all I could smoke that night
Was my trusted Pall Malls
They were comforting in this strange place

I could see the bannister make that weird curve
In that shadowy stairway
The rail continued on up into the dark
Out of sight
If it hadn't been for that little window
On the cold side of the house
There might be no light at all
I had to pee

I knew I could climb those steps
First I had to find my legs
Then I'd find the courage to turn the corner
I had asked several times where the little room was
I know now, all I had to do was follow the smell

The capped gas line
In the unused fireplace
Looked like a lonely knight
Standing in the corner of a castle dungeon
The hearth was full of dust
Damp stains and cobwebs
God only knows what torture took place there

The Judge's picture sat proud on the mantel
Two candle sentries stood unlit-quiet
Worn-tired
I looked at the clock
I had to pee

Allie handed me another cold one
As I tilted my head back in a long gulp
I noticed a picture on a dark wall
The frame appeared to be made from scrap lumber
By an amateur with a hatchet
And a lot of Elmer's glue
But it was the strange little man
That was peeking from inside the covered bridge

That held my attention
I looked across the river
There was a dirt road that went up over a hill
A barbed wire fence ran up one side of the road
And an open pasture was on the other side
At the top of the hill a driveway
Lined with old sweet gum trees
Led up to a quaint little mint green house
In back was a full silo
And a barn that was half painted red
Two dogs happily chased a boy toward the river
I looked back to the bridge
And the peeking man was gone

I felt like a fool
As I followed Tru up the stairs
At the top he turned to the left
Reached into the darkness
A bathroom appeared
A glowing bulb hung from an old black electric cord
That was attached to a pealing sealing
A frayed shoestring was tied to a short chain
The light swayed slowly
Causing strange shadows
To jump from every nook and cranny

As Tru disappeared
He told me not to flush
He would take care of it later
Whatever that meant?
Standing over the stool
I tried to hit on the stained enamel
At the edge of the rancid water
It didn't stir the cesspool as much
And kept the noise at a minimum
The stink dug at my nostrils
Loosening my sinus
Burning my eyes
My senses wanted to run away
But I had to finish my business
I had to stay the course

An army of roaches
Peeked from the changing shadows
Eagerly waiting for the chain to be pulled
An occasional soldier
Would stray from the forces

Probably a diversionary tactic

I promised myself
I would never come here again
Without a can of air freshener
And maybe some Raid
After I shook off the visit
I returned to the stairs
From this angle the shadows
Leaned the other way
I descended easily
Returned to the sprung sofa
All eyes were staring at me
As I sat back down
I took a glance to see if I left a wet spot
On my patched bell bottoms

I slid back deep in the sofa and my defenses
My critical eye could see a dying plant
In the dining room window
They looked a lot like the winter oaks outside
They still had a lot of brown leaves yet to fall
I thought I saw a boy and girl
Sitting in the branches
They giggled
As they pointed at me

I heard a scrap and a rushing sound
I turned to see a pale yellow flame
Reach up from a blue fire
That wrapped around the end of a wooden match
It was placed below a funny little cigarette
The fire grabbed at the skinny end
And an orange-red glow moved up the yellow paper
As Patsy handed it to me

Stained Glass Souls

A strong sulfur smell mixed with a pleasant pungent aroma
Of the dried leaves
I almost sneezed
And passed it on without a toke
Tru was back picking out seeds
Allie was showing off her rose tattoo
That was etched kinda high on her left breast
I just laughed at the absurdity of this whole ordeal

I looked at the clock again
The hands didn't seem to be moving
I was afraid we might get caught in another time zone
So I got Allies attention with a cough
Gave her a pleading look
And asked her if she was ready to roll
We fought off the anchors to the couch
Then ambled to the door
We said our good-by's
And as I tried to figure out which car was mine
I felt great relief to know
I got out before I had to pee again

A Korean War Casualty

The Karo syrup oozed
As mom carefully wrote her
Brother's name on my pancake

Was this my way of honoring my Uncle Walt?

Maybe seeing him disappear
With each sweet bite
Brought his unseen death to life
Giving meaning to the
Past few days of turmoil

My four year old mind
Bewildered more than hurt
Felt the families pain more than the loss
The loss of a marine
Cut in half by a machine gun

The rifle salute
Echoed through my body
And off the headstones
Triggering an impish excitement
Down to my young bones

Today hearing taps
Can cause pride to resonate
Through my sorrow

Bottomless Boxes

Blameless bottles in bottomless boxes
Stand like statues of soldiers
Corralled next to stacks of newspaper and magazines
Shallow reminders of how
History repeats itself till
We can no longer breathe in the dust
And moldy air of the stored forgotten

Ages of cobwebs catches
The bookworms
The philosophers
The dreamers
That are collected for multi-legged devourers
Needing our blood-
Our brains-
Our genetic clingings
All the while the old wine bottle army
Waits in the cardboard forts
As the open necks force me
To think of drunken wanderings
And released genies

The sour and sweet residue
In those fragile containers
Just dried-up folly
Next to my fermented residue

That still stains my mind and greases my ego

Deep Freeze

Like arms raised
Above a crowd
The grass waves
Atop the cold Stark snow

Green in my reality
I reach past
Frozen white ways
In dreams I extend
Beyond my covers

Ready for the thaw

Sitting on a Cabin Porch at the Foot of an Old Mountain

There's a blue jay scolding something as usual
I hear a woodpecker somewhere pecking wood
There's a scurrying chipmunk with cheeks stuffed full
An unseen unknown bird is singing darn good
Dogwood and sumac are blazing a trail
As sweet gum and maple deal a royal flush
Deer feed cautiously flicking their tails
And squirrels gather in a playful rush
I hear a kid calling for grandpa
Probably their last picnic of the cooling year
It's hard to believe it's already fall
Glad I took time to spend some of it here

Delicate Threads

Stars strung on delicate threads hang like memories

Live jewels of experience comedy and pain
Doors and windows to our existence
We can hate or love or see things as they are
Rhinestones and diamonds glittering gates

Come with me to the edge of soil and stone
Come
Out where the air and water meet the land
Out where the ground erodes and
Rocks are polished like precious gems
Where wind and waves smooth jagged desires

Out here

The only possible chance for fire is sheltered
Smoldering in our hearts
Protected where the elements come together

Out here

Where we hang on delicate threads ...

THE DINER

I saw him touch her
A gentle stroke across her shoulder
Did she even notice?
So common
Did she accept the caring?
A nonchalant transference of energy
Did she feel it;
Even unconsciously?

I caught this out of the corner of my eye
I'm glad I was paying attention
So often I'm only seeing the offenses
The fear
The anger

His gentle electricity searched for her circuits
A direct current from his casual affection
Maybe it took this stranger's glance
To acknowledge the importance of this moment
Did they know they were making life easier?
Just ordinary caring

Ordinary!
There is nothing ordinary about love

Isn't this what we are searching for?
So we can get past the intricate network
Of humanities
Tribal posturing
Ritual erasing
Children raising children

Donald Queen

Individual dams of potential
Controlled release can light a city
Raging forth
It can destroy the same city
Our daily rain or run off
Can generate energy
Or fracture walls in emotional devastation

It's funny how I saw this out of the corner of my eye
I'm glad I was paying attention!

Causeways

I was sitting in the shade, because yesterday's fun at Coco Beach had me red and sore. The cool air off the Indian River reminded me of my Midwestern home and the fact that it is February, not an early summer day. I watched the gulls exchange seats on the remnants of an old dock. They chatted at each other like it was normal behavior. A little blue heron worked its way over rocks and concrete rubble on the shore line. Its long beak on the end of it's snakelike, neck would disappear often in the crevices. And just as he was moving out of sight behind some bushes, a shadow caused me to look over my shoulder. On top of a telephone pole, a very large bird was placing a palm leaf in the biggest nest I'd ever seen. I grabbed my binoculars and watched the bird's long wings grab the air in slow powerful thrusts. I watched until it disappeared behind the many trees.

I looked back to the river and the gulls continued with their occasional pitiful cries, and I thought about the causeway in the distance. I laughed about how I couldn't figure out what Aunt Marge was calling those high humped bridges. A new word like causeway and Aunt Marge's New England accent made it difficult to understand what she was talking about. She went on to tell us in her special way that these high, humped bridges allowed the water traffic and the cars to flow uninterrupted.

A pelican floated by and I wondered how something so goofy looking on the ground could look so majestic in the air? And how can something look so awkward and graceful at the same time. And how do I say motionless but moving? I heard a splash and looked to my left to see a large bird rise above the water. It hesitated in the air then climbed circling closer to me. As it searched the waves it suddenly stopped, folded its wings in and dropped like a missile into the water. For a moment it was totally submerged. Then just as fast as it entered, the dripping bird flew back out. The bird climbed about ten feet, stopped and with wings still spread it shuddered comically, shaking the water from its feathers. It then flew on to circle further away from me. At a distance I watched as the diver went through the same routine. I couldn't tell if it was catching anything but I was certainly getting something from it. Researching later in Aunt Marge's bird book I found that this bird, just a little smaller than a bald eagle was an osprey.

Still in awe of the close encounter with the osprey I watched a long, sleek cabin cruiser cut a vee down the middle of the channel, just a short distance from a muddled area in the blue-green river. In this shallow place a great blue heron stood like a tree limb stuck in the mud. I scanned other curiosities in the area and when I looked back, the great blue had a fish in or on its beak. From my distance I couldn't see how the heron managed to eat its catch, but a few smaller birds were moving in to get a closer look.

The small waves continued to push against their boundaries and the wind rustled the palms in the salty air. Off to my right about fifty yards or so, a small boat bobbed and swayed as the water slapped against its blue paint. Its motion reminded me of a child dancing anxiously, ready to play. The mast rocked naked except for a few ropes hanging from the top.

A small car pulled close to me and parked. The two occupants seemed more concerned with their conversation than the wonderful surroundings. As I watched a bee buzz near my feet, a large panel truck pulled in with speakers throbbing. The bee moved to another cluster of yellow flowers. I climbed into my forest-green van to find another sweet spot. As I drove down the curvy, narrow Indian River road, I slid by the spiked palm trees and wandered how long it takes for the grayish-green Spanish moss to grow in those long, drooping clumps on the strong limbs of the live oak trees.

Blame It On the Hot Coffee

Wisp of fog drift from my cup
Lifting dull eyes clouding my aches
How many mornings left to wake up?
One at a time is all I can take
I blow at my thoughts
Take a sip
Wonder if I gave a damn
Wrestle the paper to the comic strip
Gnaw on cold toast
Dripping jam

PALE DREAMS

I had death on my hands

I brushed the coarse ashes from my fingertips

The young wind swirled gray powder
As the bag was emptied on the rough boulder
Light flakes floated to nothing
The water gradually lunged forward toward the heavier remains

Crumbled leftovers of youthful dreams
Brought home to mingle and blend into the patterns of another day
Another way to coexist with our earthly realm
Brought home to ease worn hearts and strengthen family ties

The waves inched up the fractured boulder
Giving the honored one's time to think about change
Time to mingle and blend the thoughts and feelings and tears

I watched a small fishing boat move from cage trap to cage trap
Looking for today's sustenance

The waves lulled me into quietness
Gradually crawling
Then crashing beyond their usual distance
They leaped to test new ground
Then pulled back to grow again
Damp salty air eased in and out of my lungs
I listened and watched and thought about transition
About life with loved ones
About peace and suffering
I watched the dark shape of a cormorant skim the swells
I heard gulls cry in the distance

Stained Glass Souls

A wave jumped farther than before to grab at the ashes
Taking them down the rocks
Pulling them back into the harbor
Unnumbered slaps of water
Left just a few damp granules looking like pale sand
One last reach from the rising tide

And the hard shore was washed clean

We hugged each other
Then found memory stones
For the loved ones that couldn't make it to this special good-by

THE FLOWER

We were at Aunt Mary's
Mom was sitting with her at the dinner table
They were probably waiting for
Dad and Uncle Everett to come back
From some alcoholic related activity

All the other kids were probably asleep
Sea Hunt was on the little black and white-
Being a rerun I wanted something to do-

I found a Bible on the little book case
I hoped it had pictures
The first colorful print made me peek
Over my shoulder at Mom
There were two bodies
Strategically placed behind bushes
And the woman's long hair
I almost didn't see the snake hanging
From a fruit tree

On another page a man in a large boat
With a lot of animals floated on stormy waves
Next, a group of people were walking across
The bottom of the sea
There were two walls of water held back
By the magic of a long-haired old man
With arms raised to the sky
The other pictures faded from my memory
When I came to the ones
With a man walking on water
And three men nailed on wooden crosses

Stained Glass Souls

But, the thing I remember most in that book
Was the flattened red flower
That I sneakily plucked a petal from
The feint sweet smell
And the hint of softness
From that dead blossom
Still lives in me today

Habits

Born on an island in a raging sea
She stood too long on her bitter pain
Not sure anymore who she wanted be
Thought she had nothing left to gain

Her joy was buried deep in yesterday
She was too serious for her brothers
So all the boys had quietly run away
And she gave up on those strange lovers

Long past self-pity, old ways shattered
She dove head first into the murk
No expectations, nothing mattered
Thought that life was the devils work

Gone from her isle with the maddening howl
Where habits made her one of the slaves
An eagle swooped snagging her cowl
Pulling her from the deadly waves

Tomorrow will never show its face
At least she's out of yesterday
And the view is good from this place
Soaring high above the worldly play

Lady, there's no more time for maybes
The eagle's talons have a firm hold
We're better off food for his babies
Than drowning in the thrashing cold

EBB and Flow

I sit on your shore
The gentle waves gradually move closer
They ebb and flow like they are unsure
They pull back and leave debris
Shells hauled from the deep
Are scattered in the wane

And as I talk to your sun sparkled eyes
You soothe my undertow
That draws me back
To the cold dark depths of insanity

I begin to design castles
Wondering how your water
Acts as a glue to hold together
The tiny particles of ages
I scoop and pat
Trying to impress with my abilities
When the same thing
That holds the sand together
Comes back to flatten the castles
Spreading them to eternity

Whole kingdoms crumble
I am left with sand dropping from my fingers
Like the tight spot on an hourglass
And I wrestle with my thoughts
On how you can be so cruel

Donald Queen

Then your gentle waves come
And soothe me again
Helping me feel and know
That this moment
Is the only reality

GOD

BY ANY OTHER NAME

IS STILL GOD

THE LIE

Sometimes darkness helps me see
Though the glow of the cool moon
Or haloed street light may be
A lane to penetrate the gloom

Even with the highway's drone
Or the occasional boundary bark
I can dive to misery's deepest stone
So hard to find at noon's high mark

Do I play with it? Curse it?
Perhaps forgiveness brings me peace
Tossing and turning a restless fit
Only strangles my hope for release

So I look the monsters in the lie
They rattle chains, moan and groan
Wanting me to hide-to die
let them know I'm not alone

A quiet gaze out a midnight window
The cricket's mantra begins to seep
To calm my chest, let dread go
To ease the screams-to sleep

PEEKING THOMAS

I've seen you peeking from behind the trees
Looking over the walls, dancing in my dreams
I've felt you luring the scattered crowd
I've heard your calls, though others be too loud
But, you patiently wait for the cries to cease,
For the lies to fall, for the reluctant release
You know I'll wake-up and end the search
Climb down off that perch giving you a chance
I feel you tinkering with my heart
Preparing another start
Dodging my won'ts and can'ts

But, what's your name?

Dripping to the Flow

There is a drop
An endless drip
That continually has to flow
Upon the vastness of our lives
That some think they can stop
They slow the Truth
That is born in us
With worldly cues
We distort with manipulations

I try to look with a Godly glance
And see the power in the dance
And see the matters of this chance
And wonder if the ripples die
Again I try with a Godly eye
And unwrap
These layers of years of ignored moments
I begin to unwind all these fears
And still can't see past the made-up lies

Peace, be still!
Peace, be still!
Love's always here-
Always here to understand
To awaken us from nightmare fortification
And open us to Godly eyes
Teach us to sing these songs of joy
To hear the ring of the silent bell
That ripples through our home made hell
Till we become one and two and all together
To become you and me and us forever
Looking through these Godly eyes

Watching life as it drips
A perpetual knowing through our hearts

God is Love
God is Love
And endless chance

So listen through the Spiritual I
Let your old self drop and die
That's all it's good for anyway
Let the moment in you see
Let the Godly in you sing
Let Spirit bring in a breath
All these wonders you can't conceive
All these miracles in this moment

God in a Box

I found God today teetering on the shelf with my books
I had sensed something and saw the box
Just before it fell away from the dusty tomes
I could see a dim light through the hinges
I put my old skeleton key in the lock
Corroded shut
What a shame
I shook the box and called to God
There was no answer
Silence-
What have I done?

I shook the box

Nothing-
I stepped past my ego
Past my guilt
Shattering the shell
I breathed in the essence of Power
I lowered my head on clasped hands
Whispering something about forgiveness
Tears washed over my knuckles
I was baptized by my sincerity
My once Awesome God had been put away
I had shoved Him up there with all that knowledge-
My ego had struck again
I had locked God away in the confines of my fear
All those rules and limitations
Had left me to fend for myself in a made-up world
Now that I'm re-aware
I share my breath with the Universe
Not just dusty corners of my room

Donald Queen

Renewed by an open mind and heart
And washed by my surrender
I can again be One in the
Glory of a new day
Far beyond a limited God I had put away
In a box
On the shelf

THE ANGEL'S PRIZE

The Angel carried a radiant star
Had both hands full of the glow
Yet the Messenger didn't know
That it's light could shine so far

Near the gate at the guide post
The Boss said to soar high
So the Angel took to the sky
Being one with the Glorious Host

So few see the feathered wings
Though some may see the light
Slowly moving across the night
Much higher than our reasoning's

We often wander alone in the dark
For the city lights born of men
Wash out the brilliance of Heaven
Sometimes causing us to miss the mark!

The star guides the humble-wise
Gives hope to the teachable herd
We listen for the inner words
And hunger for the Angel's Prize

I Am

I Am as close as a thought from you
As close as a breath drawing in
As close as the blood running through
And as close as clasping a stranger's hand

I Am as close as seeds on a farm
As close as winter's numbing cold
As close as a baby in your arms
Close as a dream that will unfold

As close as nature on a walk
Or the stream you splash in
As close as the motive when you talk
As close as your latest little sin

I Am as close as a shadow on the wall
As close as whispers from the soul
A close as a moment before a fall
Or the nourishing soup in your bowl

As close as beauty on the eyes
As close as the sun or soothing rain
As close as those secret little lies
Or the buried, sat on, throbbing pain

I Am as close as a robin's broken wing
As close as a smile or friendly nod
Close as doing the next best thing
Close, because I Am a personal God!

A Spiritual Experience

The air is still and sticky as I chose my way down the tricky path
Loose stones keep taking my eyes off the wooded hillside
Aged shortleaf pines share their rich scent as they veil the sun
Dogwoods give a graceful balance to the rock-covered ground
While the fresh smell of new growth mingles
With the musky and sweet odors of earth and decay
I stop to watch a crouched lizard that's trying to hide
In the lichen growing on a boulder

Savoring the abundant food for my senses
I enjoy my way down to a mellow, murmuring stream
I wander back and forth, following the water
Finally noticing a path, I walk easier
To gape my way through the splendor

The heavy air seems to intensify my surroundings
Pines stand on the edge of the gash in the hard earth
Feathery ferns grow from cracks in the rock walls
The gentle gurgle of the clear water calms my tired ways
Life's struggles have no meaning on this enchanted walk

I wonder how I can stay in such a small package
Tied so neat with barbed wire
Years of frustration and anxiety surfaces in my eyes
Like the stream my tears begin to flow
As I try to walk I have one of those long sobs
That most men don't want others to know about

Unable to continue the journey
I crouch on the edge of a small boulder
Trying to see through tear-glossed eyes
I take off my shoes and socks

Then sink my soles in the soothing water
A mild breeze dries my face

A small snake races across the stream from behind a rock
Something must have disturbed his hiding place

Expectations and New Awakenings

We locked the van and headed up the narrow path at the end of the parking lot. My memories of the creek and wooded, rocky landscape brought me back once more to share its splendor. My new woman friend, Bobbie Jo was hobbling from a fall at the shut-ins on the Black River. So we walked slowly along the stream on the uneven terrain.

I was looking for the spiritual experience I had found there before. A few years ago, walking through this patch of Eden, I had been ready for a change. At that time, I wasn't thinking about who I was or what I might be seeing next. I was caught in the awe of nature. I'd say I was in the Now when I wandered into a clearing along the old creek. With all my defenses down I was lifted above my human self. The scent of the pines and clear running water, the rugged rocks and graceful dogwoods lifted my thoughts above my petty grievances. The open door to my mind let out years of rubbish, leaving room for the moment.

Now, working our way up the eroding path we watched our steps as we looked for special places I had encountered before. It was late summer and the creek wasn't as vibrant as I'd remembered. We took several breaks to rest Bobbie Jo's leg. I got more and more frustrated as we continued on. The nature was nice, but wasn't the wonderful experience I'd known before. I ran ahead looking for a path to find an easier way back for Bobbie Jo. It didn't work, nothing looked quite the same. I was disappointed at not being able to find the past. Frustrated at not finding a better path and concerned about Bobbie Jo, I kept apologizing. I felt responsible for getting lost up this creek. All I had wanted was to share a spiritual experience.

Bobbie Jo calmly told me to stop worrying. She suggested I relax and enjoy the walk. So we turned back to retrace our steps to the parking lot. Along the way I still checked the hillside for any sign of the old path. I knew it would be a better choice to get back to the van. As I ambled, I tried to convince myself that all I had to do was live not make life happen.

We had gone a while when Bobbie Jo let out a yell. I turned to see her up on her tip toes frantically, but slowly backing away. I looked where she was pointing and saw two copperheads on the side of the trail. I had been looking so hard to find the old path and so lost in my head, I had stepped right over the snakes. I had been using a small tree branch to knock down spider webs. Now I used it to move the copperheads so Bobbie Jo wouldn't have to walk through the thick brush. The larger snake moved on without any trouble. But the smaller one held her ground, determined to make her own decision. With a little more effort I was able to flip the snake far enough away to let my frantic friend pass.

Back on the trek, with my senses fine-tuned now, it wasn't long before I thought I'd detected the remnants of the old trail. Apparently it didn't get used anymore. As I walked around the area trying to make sure this was the exit I'd been looking for, I became agitated again. I was afraid to take Bobbie Jo up the hill if it might lead her into more trouble. She finally batted away my fear, saying we should go for it. After we went a short distance, the underbrush began to thin out some. Then we used the old path more as a guide than as a place to walk. Though I was still afraid for my friend, a joint effort got us steadily up the hill. Yes, we were more alert for snakes now.

At first I thought I was seeing a grandstand for an amphitheater or some kind of stadium. When I got closer, I saw picnic tables stacked for storage. They were at the end of the road I'd hoped to find. So telling Bobbie Jo of my plan to jog the mile or two back to the parking area, I headed back to where we started. I dodged the weeds growing out of the disintegrating pavement and I went right to my head again on how I had screwed this up. I pictured Bobbie Jo hobbling along in her sweaty, red shirt and blue jeans. As I ran around the gate blocking the old road, I thought of how all I wanted to do was share a special experience with someone I love. As I loped along, I realized how impressed I was with Bobbie Jo's determination and calmness in the middle of my fear and frustration.

I watched the woods as my feet hit the pavement. I read the signs that directed the visitors to the campground and picnic areas. One sign told of controlled burns to keep the forest healthy. In fact, if the underbrush hadn't been burned off, we probably wouldn't have been able to find the old path to lead us up from the creek bed. The road was mostly downhill and my spirits raised with each stride. I still took the blame for the predicament, but my ego was coming to the rescue. In no time I would be driving back to pick up my love interest.

As I neared the parking area, I saw a woman in a red shirt and blue jeans. I had run right into The Twilight Zone. Paranoia had me thinking I had been the brunt of some weird joke. Maybe the heat had gotten to me more than I had realized. I was thinking I'd been fooled again. They would have a laugh at my expense. But as I got closer I saw that the woman was not Bobbie Jo. So now I felt like the fool that I thought they were trying to make me.

Happy the van was parked in the shade, I humbly climbed into the van to hurry back to my partner. She hadn't stayed where I'd asked her to. I found her limping down the hot road looking like a wilted flower. As Bobbie Jo shut the door, she told me she had to walk, she was afraid she would find me on the road dying from heat exhaustion. Then she told me about the beautiful butterflies she had seen near the area posted for controlled burns.

ReCreation

Somewhere in this darkness
I feel the essence of life
Ready to be molded
To be kneaded and folded
In on itself tonight

I look at a connect-a-dot sky
Or reflections off a ceiling of clouds
Retrace my steps in the lies
Think that I must surely die
I pull back the layers of shrouds

My head and heart like hands
Caress the shapeless forms
Address the peaks and crevices
Choosing what my preference is
Tossing out unneeded norms

Down in the shivering fear
Pushing away the warnings
I see love can still be ours
It's the key to all the powers
It reminds what being reborn is

THE CALLING

So I'm sitting here searching an opening
A chink in the armor
A portal to let me in or let It out
I have a need to know this Something
Maybe even to connect to
Or immerse myself into this Mystic Other

I don't know if touching It would be like breaking a dam
Or just opening a door
I only know I want to understand this whatever It is more
This Something Other

But maybe . . .
Just maybe It isn't so much other, as part of me
Maybe . . . my . . . True Self?

I've been thinking lately
At wanting to connect with my True Family
Maybe this family isn't just physical

Maybe I'm seeking a Deeper or Higher Kinship
To a Calling that wants me as much as I want It
My True Family, hmmm
Maybe this True Family is what holds all This together?

Right now I can't tell if this desire is for words
Brush strokes or
Breaths of trees and rivers flowing
I don't know if I'm pining for love
Or running from the state of the world

In spite of an earthly fear

Donald Queen

I want to embrace this lush peace that Calls to me
A blush of innocence and a playful smile that can melt
All this ice that burns me

Let me breathe again!
I wonder at these thoughts
And ponder on my walks
And gaze at seas of trees and grassy hills
That wave over the greening of the season

Washing over me in a joy of right minded coalescence
I watch the lakes and streams push at their boundaries
A large carp noses through the shallows
A small family of wood ducks sneak for cover
I fuse into my little adventures
I watch humming birds flirt with the flowers
Ground hogs scurry to their hiding places
Hawks and buzzards float with the clouds
I see a jogger pass with a serene smile

I wonder if this Calling is just an illusion
Or is the illusion thinking we are separate? Hmmm . . .

And So Are We

As Spirit wound through my soul
I wondered at this mortal home
Believing life a school of sorts
I plucked an apple from the tree
I placed this offering at the altar-
Was this love or just a plea?

I've lived in sputtered, stuttered starts
Yet acted like I knew the Truth
But only guessed at all this wonder
And pined in selfish little schemes
Directed at great works around me

Now art and science intertwine
Finally joined in heart and mind
Bringing religion to its knees
Please don't throw anyone from the path
God is Love and so are we!

A Just Right Spring Day

You know those days
When you put the world
Back where it belongs?
You know, beneath your feet
Not on your shoulders

When the birds are singing
You specials songs
And you gingerly side step
Stones and awesome boulders

When each breath is a love affair
With things not held in hands
And Spring's trees and flowers
Show us how to live again-anew

Where everyplace you look
There's good people in the land
And you feel God's energy
Everywhere present
Outside-in and through

Wow,
Give me more of these!

A Soul in Disguise

Images and thoughts
Past and future
Clank by
Like box cars
I watch my breath
Hear muffled beats
A second hand slips
Up and back
Up and back

Clouds float by

You can have me
Whispers passion
Please--take me

A soul in disguise
I feel a heart throb
Savor the singing
Bleed clear crystals
Echoes send a pulse

No bad boy
No good boy
Just a pocket
Of polished stones
To toss in the pond
Liquid rhythm
Waves on the surface
Settle
Into the deep
Gently

Donald Queen

Into the deep

Quietly
Swirling
Into the deep

Enfolding

Into the deep

Printed in the United States
By Bookmasters